Goanna

Jenny Wagner

Illustrated by Noela Hills

Puffin Books

for Nina
from Noela

Puffin Books
Penguin Books Australia Ltd,
487 Maroondah Highway, PO Box 257
Ringwood, Victoria 3134, Australia
Penguin Books Ltd, Harmondsworth, Middlesex, England
Viking Penguin, A Division of Penguin Books USA Inc.
375 Hudson Street, New York, New York 10014, USA
Penguin Books Canada Limited,
10 Alcorn Avenue, Toronto, Ontario, Canada M4V 3B2
Penguin Books (NZ) Ltd,
182-190 Wairau Road, Auckland 10, New Zealand

First published 1988 by Viking
Published in Puffin, 1989

10 9 8 7 6 5 4 3

Copyright © Jenny Wagner, 1988
Illustrations copyright © Noela Hills, 1988

Made and printed in Hong Kong by Bookbuilders Ltd
Typeset in Palatino by Leader Compositon Pty Ltd

National Library of Australia
Cataloguing-in-Publication data:

Wagner, Jenny.
Goanna

ISBN 0 14 054081 4

I. Monitor lizards - Juvenile fiction. I. Hills, Noela, II. Title.
A823'.3

Goanna had lived for a very
long time, guarding an old hollow log.

The log was empty, but he guarded it just the same. He liked to pretend there was treasure inside, and if anyone came to steal it he would frizzle them with his breath.

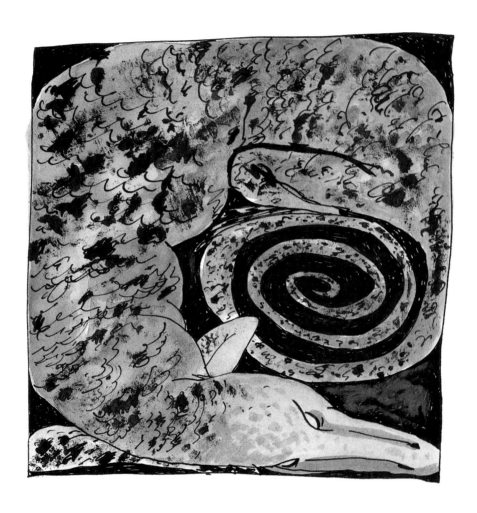

But the log stayed empty; no one ever came near, and his ordinary goanna breath wouldn't even warm his hands on cold days. So most of the time he slept.

Then one day when he was out looking for food he saw something glinting in the bushes. It was a bottle made of amber glass, and when the sun shone through, it made sunsets on his fingers.

Goanna took it home to his log and looked after it.

Next day when he was tidying up he found two more amber bottles, and after that he tidied the gully every day.

And every day he found new things. Goanna looked after everything and kept everything in its place, and when the log filled up he found new places to keep things. He made roads and valleys and mountains and on every mountain he put a treasure.

And in the evenings, when no one was around, he climbed on his highest mountain and dared his enemies to come and be frizzled.

No one ever came. It was a good life.

THIS IS THE SITE FOR A COMPLEX OF SHOPS AND OFFICES.
Planning permission applied for.

Then one morning he looked at his best mountain and saw that someone had put a sign on it.

He couldn't read it, but he felt sure it said something like 'Beware of the Goanna', and when he tidied the gully that morning he dusted the sign as well.

A few days later he awoke from a dream of underground fires to find that his log was shaking. He scrambled up. There was a roaring sound all round him, and it was coming closer.

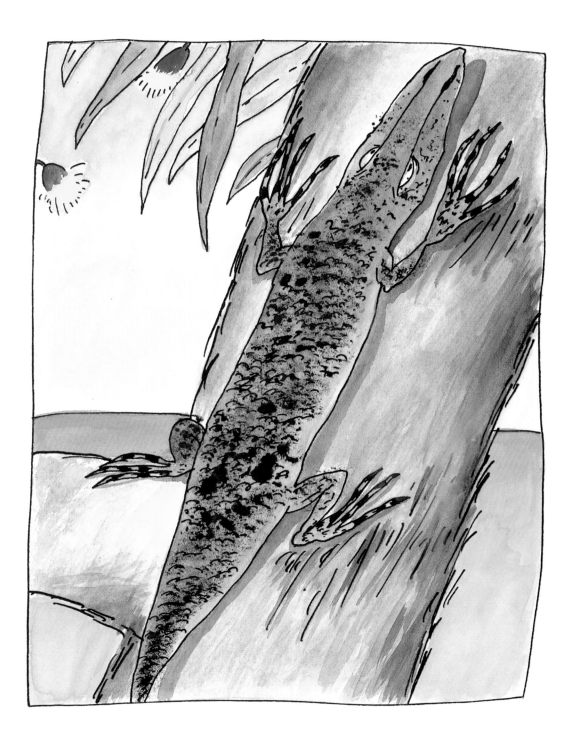

Goanna forgot about guarding things, and he forgot about frizzling his enemies. He left his treasure where it was and ran up the nearest tree.

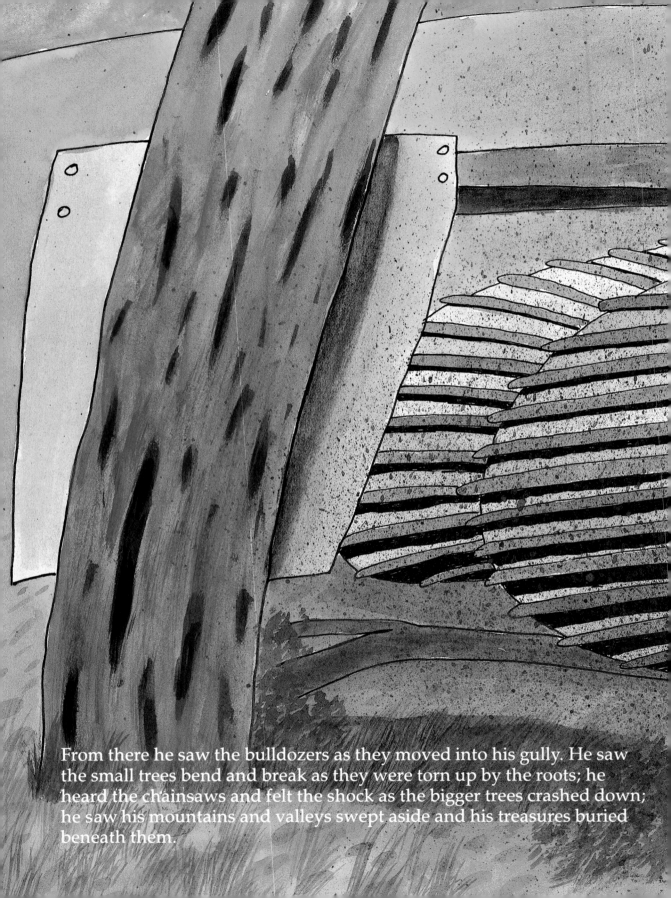

From there he saw the bulldozers as they moved into his gully. He saw the small trees bend and break as they were torn up by the roots; he heard the chainsaws and felt the shock as the bigger trees crashed down; he saw his mountains and valleys swept aside and his treasures buried beneath them.

And the bulldozers kept on coming.

Goanna left his tree and ran, and kept on running till he came to a quieter place. He curled up tight and pressed his face into the ground, but he could still hear the roar of the bulldozers and the thud of falling trees.

He stayed there for a long time, until the noise had stopped.

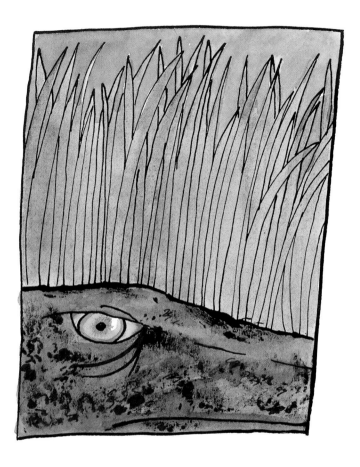

Then he went back to see what was left.

There was nothing, only concrete. Somewhere underneath it his hollow log was buried, but he had no way of telling where.

He walked along the concrete till he came to a patch of bare ground.
He scooped dead leaves together to make himself a nest, and slept.

He slept for several months. In his dreams he heard the sounds of men and machines, but he took no notice.

Then one morning he awoke and saw that he was lying next to a car park. Beyond that was a shopping complex, with trees in concrete tubs along the front.

No one had bothered about the hollow he was lying in. It was full of dry grass and tangled creeper, and weeds. And nearby on a post there was a rubbish bin.

As Goanna watched, someone aimed a bottle at the bin, and missed.
The bottle rolled down the hollow and landed at Goanna's feet.

But this one made no sunsets on his fingers; Goanna could see through
this one quite clearly.

He left it where it was and walked away.